W9-BMM-077

MY SCHOOL COMMUNITY

Portia Summers

Enslow Publishing
101 W. 23rd Street
Suite 240
New York, NY 10011
USA

enslow.com

WORDS TO KNOW

body—A whole group together.

community—A group of people who live or work together.

custodian— A person who is in charge of keeping a building or other place clean and in good shape.

immunizations—Shots that keep you from getting sick.

information—Facts, figures, stories, pictures, and numbers.

nutritious—Full of things the body needs to stay healthy.

subjects—Different things to study, like art, reading, music, or math.

CONTENTS

A school community includes the students and all of the adults who help the children learn and grow.

Working Together at School

People who live or work together are called a community. This group of people spends time together, working or doing other activities together. Members of a community try to help each other.

Communities can be as big as a whole city or as small as a single family. Schools are a kind of community. Many people are part of the school community.

The Way to School

Some students ride the bus to and from school. The bus driver picks them up at their house in the morning. He or she drops them off again when school gets out. Other children walk to school. A crossing guard or a police officer may help them cross busy streets. They all have help getting to school. The people who help are part of the school community.

The crossing guard makes sure students get to school safely. He is an important member of the school community.

The Heart of the School

At the center of every school are the students. School is the place where students come to learn and be together. There are lots of subjects that students learn at school, like reading, writing, and math. But students learn other important skills as well. At school they learn how to get along with others, both children and teachers.

All Types of Schools

At some schools all the students study science. At others they all study art. Most schools let their students study a lot of different kinds of things in one place. There are elementary schools for children. Middle schools teach older children. High schools and colleges teach young adults and adults.

Groups of Students

There are a lot of students in one school. There are a lot of students in each grade, too. Students are usually put together in classes. Usually they are placed in classes with students in their own grade. That way one teacher can help many students at once. Together all the classes in the school community are called the student body.

Working in small groups helps students share ideas and learn from each other.

What Teachers Do

We could not have schools with teachers. They play an important part in the school community. They help students learn. Teaching is not an easy job. Every student is different. The teacher has to figure out how to help every student learn.

The teacher has different ways to figure out if students are learning. Teachers give tests. They ask the class questions. They give students homework and projects. These are all ways to find out if students are learning.

What Is Your Classroom Like?

Do you have classes where you sit by yourself at your desk? How about classes where everyone sits in a circle on the floor? You may even have classes where you go outside to learn about trees and bushes and grass and vines.

The Leader of the School

Principals are the leaders of the school community. They are in charge of running the school. A principal makes sure that the teachers have everything they need to teach. He or she makes sure that the students have everything they need to learn.

The principal greets students as they arrive for a new school day.

Helping Hands

Teachers and principals are not the only important people in a school community. Some people, like the librarian, make sure that you learn everything you can. Other people, like nurses and lunchroom workers, work hard so that students stay healthy.

Read to Learn

The librarian is part of the school community. He or she is in charge of the library. The librarian helps students and teachers find information.

Librarians order books, magazines, and videos for students and teachers to borrow. They organize these things so they are easy to find.

Electronic Library

Libraries used to have to try to fit as many books and magazines as they could into their library. Now librarians can use computers to find information from all over the world. The Internet is like one giant library.

The librarian's job is to get students excited about reading and learning.

Health and Safety

The school nurse has many different jobs. Students can get sick or hurt. The nurse makes them feel better. He or she can decide if the student needs to go home or to the doctor.

Nurses can help students take medicine. They also make sure that all the students have had their immunizations.

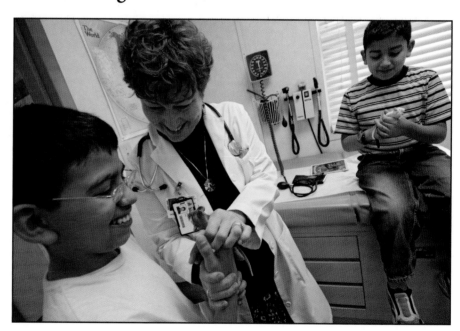

Balanced Meals

The lunchroom worker is another part of the school community. A full day of learning takes a lot of energy. Students need to eat a nutritious meal. This will keep their minds working hard. Lunchroom workers cook and serve lunch to the students. They make sure that the food is prepared in a way that is healthy and tasty.

Everybody Has a Part to Play

Teachers and principals, bus drivers and parents, lunchroom workers and custodians are all important members of the school community. They help students learn. They make sure children get to school safely, and they keep the building clean. Students have a job to do, too. They help make school a safe, healthy place where everyone can learn to be his or her best.

Students work together on a science project. Being part of a school community means doing your best and helping others.

21

ACTIVITY: MY SCHOOL HELPERS

As you learned in this book, there are many helpers in a school community. Let's explore who helps you in your own school.

1. Copy the circle chart from p. 23.

2. In the middle oval, write your own name.

3. In each of the outer circles, write the name and job of someone who helps you in school.

4. By each person's name, write one sentence about how that person helps you. (One has been done for you as an example.)

5. Look at your completed chart. There are lots of people who help you in your school community. Who do you help at school?

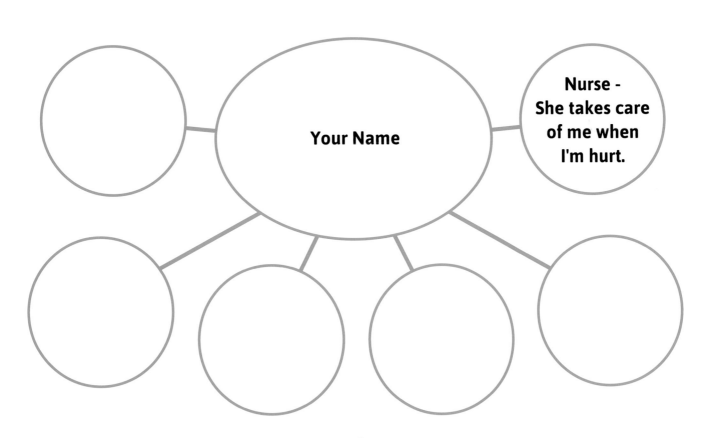

Your Name

**Nurse -
She takes care
of me when
I'm hurt.**

LEARN MORE

Books

Edwards, Clint. *Show Me Community Helpers.* Mankato, MN: Capstone, 2013.

Hunter, Rebecca. *Teacher.* Twickenham, England: Tulip Books, 2014.

Kreisman, Rachelle. *People Who Help: A Kids' Guide to Community Helpers.* South Egremont, MA: Red Chair Press, 2015.

Murray, Julie. *Librarians.* Edina, MN: Abdo, 2015.

Websites

KIds Discover
www.kidsdiscover.com/teacherresources/schools-around-the-world/
Read about different school communities around the world.

Enchanted Learning
www.enchantedlearning.com/themes/communityhelpers.shtml
Complete fun activities to learn more about the helpers in our communities.

INDEX

Published in 2017 by Enslow Publishing, LLC.
101 W. 23rd Street, Suite 240, New York, NY 10011
Copyright © 2017 by Enslow Publishing, LLC
All rights reserved.

No part of this book may be reproduced by any means without the written permission of the publisher.

Library of Congress Cataloging-in-Publication Data
Names: Summers, Portia.
Title: My school community / Portia Summers.
Description: New York : Enslow Publishing, 2017 | Series: Zoom in on communities | Audience: K to Grade 3. | Includes bibliographical references and index.
Identifiers: ISBN 978-0-7660-7827-7 (library bound) | ISBN 978-0-7660-7824-6 (pbk.) | ISBN 978-0-7660-7826-0 (6 pack)
Subjects: LCSH: Schools--Juvenile literature. | Classrooms--Juvenile literature. | Communities--Juvenile literature.

Classification: LCC LB1513.S96 2017 | DDC 371--dc23
Printed in Malaysia

To Our Readers: We have done our best to make sure all website addresses in this book were active and appropriate when we went to press. However, the author and the publisher have no control over and assume no liability for the material available on those websites or on any websites they may link to. Any comments or suggestions can be sent by e-mail to customerservice@enslow.com.

Photo Credits: Cover, p. 1, p. 13 wavebreakmedia/Shutterstock.com; graphics throughout Kev Draws/Shutterstock.com (people circle), antoshkaforever/Shutterstock.com (people holding hands), 3d_kot/Shutterstock.com (houses); p. 4 Thomas Barwick/Iconica/Getty Images; p. 7 Andersen Ross/Blend Images/Getty Images; p. 9 mediaphotos/iStock; p. 11 Steve Debenport/E+/Getty Images; p. 14 Sean Locke/Shutterstock.com; p. 17 kali9/E+/Getty Images; p. 18 Karen Kasmauski/RGB Ventures/SuperStock/Alamy; p. 19 Cathy Yeulet/Thinkstock; p. 21 Richard G. Bingham II/Alamy, p. 22 Evellean/Shutterstock.com.